W9-BGA-125

NEA
EARLY CHILDHOOD
EDUCATION SERIES

Multicultural Education in Early Childhood Classrooms

Edwina Battle Vold
Editor

A NATIONAL EDUCATION ASSOCIATION
P U B L I C A T I O N

Printing History
    First Printing: April 1992

Note

The opinions expressed in this publication should not be construed as representing the policy or position of the National Education Association. Materials published by the NEA Professional Library are intended to be discussion documents for educators who are concerned with specialized interests of the profession.

Library of Congress Cataloging-in-Publication Data

Multicultural education in early childhood classrooms/Edwina Battle Vold, editor.
        p. cm — (NEA Early childhood education series)
    Includes bibliographical references.
    ISBN 0-8106-0353-5
        1. Intercultural education — United States. 2. Early childhood education—United States. I. Vold, Edwina Battle. II. Series: Early childhood education series (Washington, D.C.)
    LC1099.3.M84   1992
    370.19'341—dc20

91-23796
CIP

CONTENTS

The Editor

Edwina Battle Vold is Professor of Early Childhood Education and Chair of the Department of Professional Studies in Education at Indiana University of Pennsylvania.

The Advisory Panel

Ruth Adams-Gadsden, Media Specialist and Teacher, Rose Park Middle School, Nashville, Tennessee; Child Advocate, Special Educator, and Counselor

John Delonas, Learning Consultant, Blairstown Elementary School, New Jersey

Donna B. Foglia, Kindergarten Teacher, Evergreen School District, San Jose, California

Anne Richardson Gayles, Professor of Secondary Education, Florida A&M University, Tallahassee

Jacqueline Gorrie, Kindergarten Teacher, Elizabeth Pole School, Taunton, Massachusetts

Carl A. Grant, Professor of Curriculum and Instruction, University of Wisconsin-Madison

Shelton Gunaratne, Associate Professor of Mass Communications, Moorhead State University, Minnesota

Barbara J. Schram, Kindergarten Teacher, Grand Ledge Public Schools, Michigan

John G. Taylor, Professor, Department of Elementary and Secondary Education, Murray State University, Kentucky

Elaine P. Witty, Dean, School of Education, Norfolk State University, Virginia

Rosalind Lucille Yee, Specific Language and Reading Development Specialist, Prince George's County Public Schools, Maryland

PREFACE

This monograph is both a rationale for multicultural education and a how-to manual. It includes activities and strategies for teaching preschool and primary-age children from a multicultural perspective.

The work of each contributor typifies what happens in an early childhood environment that highlights the processes inherent in creating an early childhood curriculum with a multicultural perspective. Each chapter contains an introductory statement that helps readers understand the importance of using a multicultural perspective in their specific areas of expertise. In each area—social studies, reading and writing, mathematics, science, and play—the authors have provided sample lessons.

The authors believe that the activities are developmentally appropriate and applicable to all types of classrooms—those with monocultural populations (all white ethnic groups, all African Americans, all Polynesians, or all members of a specific Native-American group) and those with heterogeneous racial, ethnic, and socioeconomic groups. Though some activities may refer to specific ethnic or racial groups, creative teachers can adapt them to the children in their classrooms.

Readers are encouraged to review Chapter 1, "Determining the Multicultural Curriculum," before reviewing and using the curriculum activities in the next five chapters. This introductory chapter provides the rationale for multicultural education as a holistic orientation incorporating content and processes that interact with young children's development within a social/cultural context. The final section of the monograph contains a sampling of multicultural education teacher resources.

In summary, this monograph suggests ways for teachers to make the early childhood classroom a place that provides all children with curricula that offer equal opportunities to acquire knowledge and to develop a sense of belonging and empowerment.

—Edwina Battle Vold

Chapter 1

DETERMINING THE MULTICULTURAL CURRICULUM

by Leslie R. Williams, Associate Professor of Early Childhood Education, Teachers College, Columbia University

This short philosophical essay forms the basis for inquiry into what a multicultural curriculum is and why it is a way to respond to the needs of an increasing culturally diverse population. The author expertly weaves a developmental theory and differing multicultural education goals into a set of principles of reality for teaching young children.

What makes a curriculum multicultural? The answer to this question may at first seem obvious. Closer examination of underlying issues makes it less so, however. Many curriculum developers around the United States are seeking ways to respond to the growing cultural diversity in the populations they serve; as they do so, they are beginning to unravel some of the complexities inherent in active recognition of plurality of experience.

In past years, some curriculum makers have focused on the structure of particular bodies of knowledge (such as science, social studies, or art) or sets of skills (such as beginning reading) as the substance of curriculum (Bruner 1968). Others have drawn the attention of educators to learner characteristics (cognitive, social, or physical development) as determinants of curriculum (Hohmann, Banet, and Weikart 1979), and to the contexts (individual, group, class, school, family, and community) that interact with development and thus potentially affect the learning process (Bruner 1973; Shulman 1986). The former have understood curriculum to be *content* that the learner is to absorb. The latter have viewed curriculum as a *process* through which the learner might acquire or construct knowledge.

A third group of curriculum makers has sought to combine these two perspectives in relation to philosophic or political aims. Their focus has been on producing a particular kind of person through the medium of the educational experience (Dewey 1958, 1975; Bruner 1973). The intended outcomes were, for example, responsible citizens within a democratic society, or persons able to resist substance abuse, or problem-solving, critical thinking individuals.

Most curriculum making in multicultural education has been allied with this third approach. Choosing to recognize that human experience is not identical across cultures and that both learning and subsequent behavior are influenced by culture implies a philosophic stance. When curriculum makers extend that recognition to a vision of how that reality affects the inner structures of a given society, they assume a political stance as well.

In one form or another, multicultural curriculum development has been going on in the United States for about 40 years. Early program efforts in the 1950s reflected social and political changes toward equality of opportunity, with a curriculum focus on racial relations. Those programs were joined in the 1960s and 1970s by curricula designed specifically to address the depressed academic performance of many culturally and linguistically distinct groups in the public schools, and by ethnic studies programs aimed at building the self-esteem of populations previously neglected in the curriculum. While the earlier programs were intended as an enrichment for children of all groups, the latter were often designed with remediation in mind. Even when the attempt of the latter was to involve a broad sampling of students, the public perception was that such programs were not needed for populations that appeared to be doing well with the standard school curriculum (Sleeter and Grant 1987; Vold 1989).

8

From the mid-1970s onward, new program designs began to appear that had some of the elements of the earlier intergroup relations work of the 1950s, but moved beyond that singular aim to positive recognition of cultural pluralism. These programs were once again designed for all children; they were grounded in the assumption that with increased awareness of others would come acceptance and constructive use of differences. A small number of curriculum developers, however, have challenged that fundamental assumption. These "social reconstructionists" contend that confrontation of the deep structures of society that perpetuate inequality is the only way to create lasting change. Until racism, sexism, ageism, and other forms of oppression are defeated and societal resources are redistributed, old patterns of discrimination will recur. The social reconstructionist curricula therefore aim at promoting activism toward those ends (Sleeter and Grant 1987; Vold 1989).

Multicultural curricula and programs representing all five of the aims described briefly above are now available. In addition to representing different philosophic and political positions, they also have been influenced to varying degrees by the content/process debate noted earlier that characterizes the curriculum field in general. In the case of multicultural curricula, the debate revolves around the definition of culture. When culture is understood to be a body of traditions, customs, and practices, the history or the knowledge of a people, the resulting curricula tend to focus heavily on the cultural content of one or more groups. When culture is seen as a continuing creation of a people, building on a past and moving toward a future, the resulting curricula are more process-oriented.

Allied with this debate is discussion of whether to regard the study of cultures as a separate subject in a school curriculum, or whether to integrate awareness of the influence of culture into all areas of study. In some school systems, multicultural education as the study of a cultural group continues to be seen as a subject or program. In other systems, multicultural education is seen not as a contained program, but as a perspective that is assumed regardless of the subject being taught (Ramsey 1987; Williams, De Gaetano, Harrington, and Sutherland 1985).

When multicultural education is regarded as a subject or program, the content of the program (the choice of the specific cultures to be included) is often a key issue. The inclusion of two or more cultures, to permit a basis for discussion of similarities and differences, is most important. Without such comparison, the program cannot be multicultural.

When multicultural education is regarded as a perspective, inclusiveness in the integration with other subject areas becomes the key issue. First, as a perspective, certain elements must be present to ensure authority and value. The curriculum should draw from more than one tradition to identify the elements of the subject area. Second, the examples used to illustrate the principles taught should relate to the experiences children bring with them to the classroom. These examples should recognize the children's frames of reference and help them relate new learnings to their prior knowledge. Third, the teaching strategies used should account for the several ways that children acquire or construct new knowledge and skills. Fourth, the children should be engaged in the comparison and contrast of their experience across groups as they work with any subject area, so that not only similarities but also differences in experience are considered. Finally, children should be guided toward recognition of the underlying issues in society that influence each of the preceding four dimensions of their learning.

It is the position of the authors represented in this monograph that the second approach—that is, seeing multicultural education as a perspective that should be integrated throughout all subject areas—more accurately represents current understandings of the ways in which knowledge is acquired or constructed by young children. In addition, the notion of learning or the construction of knowledge as primarily a social process offers support for the integration of a multicultural perspective throughout the early childhood curriculum. For children to learn, they must derive meaning from what is taught.

Their experiences have been embedded in social exchange within their own cultural groups, and their frames of reference reflect the shared meanings and experiences of those groups. In order for them to acquire or construct new knowledge, the new must be placed in relation to that which is already known and meanings must be renegotiated to "make sense." Providing a multicultural perspective across subject areas allows children to connect the unfamiliar with the familiar in nonthreatening ways.

A curriculum is multicultural, then, when it recognizes diversity in experience and the relationships between differences in experience and the ways children acquire or construct new knowledge. A curriculum is multicultural when it draws upon two or more traditions and ways of viewing the world, thus enabling children to recognize their prior knowledge in what is being taught. A curriculum is multicultural when to reach its educational ends it assumes a philosophic and/or political position toward creating individuals who can accept and use diversity constructively. The chapters in this monograph offer ways educators today may begin to approach such aims through specific subject areas in the early childhood curriculum.

REFERENCES

Bruner, J. S. *Toward a Theory of Instruction*. New York: W. W. Norton, 1968.

———. *The Relevance of Education*. New York: W. W. Norton, 1973.

Dewey, J. *Philosophy of Education (Problems of Men)*. Totowa, N.J.: Littlefield, Adams, 1958, 1975.

Donaldson, M. *Children's Minds*. New York: W. W. Norton, 1978.

Hohmann, M.; Banet, B.; and Weikart, D. *Young Children in Action*. Ypsilanti, Mich.: High Scope Press, 1979.

Piaget, J. *The Origins of Intelligence in Children*. New York: International Universities Press, 1952.

Ramsey, P. G. *Teaching and Learning in a Diverse World: Multicultural Education for Young Children.* New York: Teachers College Press, 1987.

Shulman, L. "Paradigms and Research Programs in the Study of Teaching: A Contemporary Perspective." In *Handbook of Research on Teaching,* edited by M. C. Wittrock, 3–36. 3d ed. New York: Macmillan, 1986.

Sleeter, C. E., and Grant, C. A. "An Analysis of Multicultural Education in the United States." *Harvard Education Review* 57 (1987): 421–44.

Vold, E. B. "The Evolution of Multicultural Education: A Socio-Political Perspective." In *Multicultural Education: A Source Book,* edited by P. G. Ramsey, E. B. Vold, and L. R. Williams. New York: Garland, 1989.

Vygotsky, L. S. *Thought and Language.* Cambridge, Mass.: M.I.T. Press, 1962.

Williams, L. R.; De Gaetano, Y.; Harrington, C. C.; and Sutherland, I. R. *ALERTA: A Multicultural, Bilingual Approach to Teaching Young Children.* Menlo Park, Calif.: Addison-Wesley, 1985.

Chapter 2

SOCIAL STUDIES THAT IS MULTICULTURAL

by Patricia G. Ramsey, Associate Professor of Psychology and Education, Mount Holyoke College

This chapter provides a rationale for the present social studies structure from kindergarten through third grade. The author discusses ways to modify typical lessons within that structure to embody a multicultural perspective. She also cautions readers about potential pitfalls in the traditional presentation of culture-related concepts.

We are both social and individual beings, connected with others in a multitude of ways, as well as ultimately alone in the world.

—W. Damon 1983

Traditionally early childhood social studies curricula have been organized around the structure of expanding environments. Typically the sequence is as follows. In kindergarten the focus is on the self, including self-concept, physical attributes, and skills and interests. First graders learn about families and their school. In the second grade, social studies is oriented toward the immediate neighborhood. In the third grade, the curriculum focuses on the children's community, including community workers, government, history, and different neighborhoods. Along with the expanding environments, patriotism is also a theme. Usually these teachings consist of learning the pledge of allegiance and national anthems, and celebrating traditional holidays that mark events in the history of the United States (e.g., Washington's birthday).

The rationale for this organization of the curriculum is developmental: young children most easily understand information that is concrete and immediate. Only as they get older are they able to comprehend facets of the world that they have not directly experienced. In some respect these assumptions reflect sound developmental theory; concrete operational children cannot think in the abstract and cannot grasp information that has no connection with their own lives. However, children can appreciate and use unfamiliar information if they learn it in a concrete and meaningful way. Moreover, exposure to unfamiliar ways of life can help them see their own lives and communities more clearly by contrasting them with the experiences of other people. These comparisons often raise questions that force children to challenge their assumptions. For example, if rural children see pictures of urban neighborhoods and read stories about children of their age who live there, they will become conscious of the distinctive attributes of their own neighborhoods. At the same time, they may gain some awareness that certain experiences and feelings are shared by all children. Thus, far from being developmentally inappropriate, the inclusion of unfamiliar material can stimulate children's understanding of their own lives and social environment.

One problem with the traditional focus on familiar life experiences is that it sets a pattern of seeing one's own lifestyle and community as the norm by which to measure all other ways of life. Thus children learn to interpret new information by how well it matches the material that is familiar to them. Subsequently, they are more likely to view unfamiliar cultures as inferior or perhaps as exotic, but not as viable and reasonable responses to the challenges of living in a particular environment. The theme of patriotism often supports this limited view of the world by emphasizing the positive aspects of this country, frequently in contrast to others. By refocusing discussions about the pledge of allegiance, national anthems, and history, teachers can help children recognize that all people feel loyal to their families, communities, and countries. In this way, children can learn about patriotism, not as a statement of superiority, but rather as an affirmation of that commitment.

Holidays are often used as a way of teaching history because they are concrete and meaningful to children. However, school celebrations are usually limited to events that honor the early European settlers in this country and do not represent a full picture of the history and the diverse backgrounds of our citizenry. An alternative approach is to focus on the themes common to holidays in many different cultures. Celebrations can reflect both the shared experiences of people and their diverse ways of expressing them. For example, most cultures celebrate the agricultural cycle of planting and harvesting. With a few modifications, teachers can incorporate a variety of traditions into the usual celebrations of spring and Thanksgiving (Ramsey 1979, 1987). Thus the focus on holidays can shift from celebrating particular events and the superiority of one group of people to learning more about humankind and the common-alities among different societies.

Young children cannot understand abstract concepts of justice and morality, but they are acutely aware of what is fair and unfair in their own lives. By learning about many people and the ways in which they live, they become conscious of differences in living conditions and often react strongly to economic dis-parities, particularly when they are made more concrete in stories and pictures. This kind of information also presents them with dilemmas about social and economic justice, which helps them challenge and refine their own ideas about what is fair.

SOCIAL STUDIES ACTIVITIES

The next few pages illustrate how typical social studies activities at different grade levels can be adapted to embody the goals of multicultural education. Because many social studies curricula are based on the expanding environments structure, the examples are drawn from this model. However, the modifica-tions can be made to any existing curricula. More examples of

15

how to modify specific activities are found in *Turning on Learning* (Grant and Sleeter 1989).

Kindergarten

Theme: Awareness of Our Bodies

Activity: Drawing Our Bodies

This activity is popular in many preschools and kindergartens. Usually, the objectives include

1. children's increased awareness of their bodies;

2. more appreciation for the physical attributes of their classmates;

3. development and application of skills in tracing, painting, cutting, and pasting.

Typically, this activity is done over a period of three to five days and includes the following steps:

1. Children work in pairs and draw around their partners who are lying on large sheets of paper.

2. Children paint their own tracings with appropriate hair, eye, and skin colors.

3. Children cut and glue on pieces of materials to "dress" their drawings.

Throughout these activities, teachers facilitate discussions about how children are the same and different and how each child is unique and special. The final products are often displayed on the walls and are the subject of discussion. The teacher may also initiate some guessing games to further increase children's awareness of their own and their peers' unique attributes.

Modifications

To embody a more multicultural perspective, teachers can elaborate this activity in several ways.

First, they can introduce the activity by showing pictures of people from all over the world, who represent different racial groups and wear a wide variety of clothing. They can discuss the fact that people look different, but all share some common characteristics, which are the focus of the tracing activity (i.e., all bodies have the same basic shape and body parts). If the children have questions about the different kinds of clothing they see, the teacher can help them identify reasons why they wear the clothing they do (e.g., type of activity, influence of the media) and why different climatic and living conditions may affect clothes.

Second, for the tracing part of the activity teachers can pair children who usually do not have much contact with each other. In this way, the activity serves as a vehicle for expanding children's range of social contacts and, in some cases, helps to dispel their negative assumptions about each other. Children can continue to work in pairs during the painting and "dressing" parts of the activity to increase the potential for cooperative interactions.

Third, during the tracing, teachers can encourage children to talk to each other about their similarities and differences to reiterate the concept that all people have common attributes, yet are unique.

Fourth, during the painting and "dressing," teachers can direct children's attention to the pictures they showed at the beginning of the activity to allow children to compare themselves to a wide range of people. If they are interested, children might want to include in their self-portrait some adornments and clothing that differ from their usual attire.

With these modifications teachers keep the focus of the activity on the concrete and immediate experience of the children, yet expand the children's range of knowledge, challenge their assumptions, and help them identify more clearly both their physical attributes and their choice of clothes.

First Grade

Theme: Families

Activity: Stories About Family Photographs

This activity is common in many early childhood classrooms and serves to fulfill the following objectives:

1. to foster the connection between families and schools;

2. to provide an opportunity for children to talk and write about their home lives and families;

3. to help children see the similarities and differences among their families.

The activity can continue for several days and usually includes the following steps:

1. Letters go home to parents requesting the photographs.

2. When all the photographs are available, children take turns showing pictures of their own family and describing who is in their household. This activity may occur during morning meeting time and continue over several days to be sure that it does not become repetitive and tedious.

3. Children write brief descriptions of their families.

4. Children make posters of their photographs, their descriptions, and some drawings that represent family activities.

Modifications

First, teachers can introduce the discussion about families by having children talk about what constitutes a family. They can then challenge these assumptions by showing the children photographs and reading stories about many different family constellations. One excellent resource is *Families: A Celebration of*

Diversity, Commitment, and Love (Jenness 1990). These discussions may also be reassuring to children who feel uncomfortable that their family does not fit the traditional model of a father, mother, two children, and a dog. The underlying theme of these discussions should be that families are large and small, come together in many ways, may or may not be biologically related, and are bound, not by prescribed roles, but by love and commitment. Helping children define what is most important about their families may lead them to come to this conclusion on their own.

Second, when sharing their family photographs, teachers can draw children's attention to the diversity of families in the class and also the similarities and differences between members of the same family and between different families.

Third, teachers may also expand these discussions by having children talk about where their families are from (including other regions of the country as well as other countries) and why they came. If children seem interested, teachers may also have them interview their parent(s) about recent family history. In these assignments, teachers should be careful about assuming that all family members have the same origins (e.g., in the case of international adoptions and blended families).

Fourth, teachers may also include some discussion about the parents' work to expose children to a wider range of occupations. Additional activities include having parents come in as guest speakers and arranging field trips to workplaces, particularly those that are underrepresented in most children's stories and media.

Fifth, teachers can have children work in teams to make group collages of their family photographs and stories to provide more opportunity for cooperative interactions and to stimulate more intimate conversations about how families are the same and different. As with the pairing for the tracing, these teams can be formed to promote interactions among children who do not have much contact with or knowledge of each other's families.

Second Grade

Theme: Our Neighborhood

Activity: Making a Model of the Immediate Neighborhood

This activity is popular and helps to develop the following skills and areas of knowledge:

1. orientation and mapping skills;

2. representation of three-dimensional space;

3. knowledge about the immediate neighborhood;

4. awareness of the resources in the immediate neighborhood.

This activity can take several days and usually includes the following steps:

1. The children and teacher walk around the neighborhood sketching maps and drawing in particular landmarks. These tasks may be divided up among the class.

2. Back in the classroom, children develop a comprehensive map of the area and locate major landmarks.

3. They return to the neighborhood with a Polaroid camera and take pictures of the buildings.

4. They work in teams to make a model of the neighborhood using scrounge materials such as different containers.

Modifications

First, teachers can direct children's attention to the different people who live in the neighborhood by asking them to note not only the location of buildings, but also the age, race, and gender of the people they see. Children can also keep a list of the types of jobs that people are doing and whether or not the buildings are in good repair. If the residents are willing, children can take their pictures on their second visit to the neighborhood.

Second, as they are making their initial map, the teacher can show pictures of other kinds of neighborhoods and help children articulate how they are like and unlike their own neighborhood. They can talk about how they think life may be different in these unfamiliar places and perhaps hear stories about children who live in different types of neighborhoods. These contrasting images can sharpen children's awareness of the distinctive features of their own neighborhood.

Third, as they build their model, children can add photographs of the people they met so that they may depict the neighborhood not simply as a collection of streets and buildings but also as a place in which people live and work.

Fourth, after they build their model, children can return to the neighborhood and imagine how the neighborhood would feel to a number of different people. The types of people can vary according to the specific neighborhood and the children's level of social understanding, but the goals are to develop children's skills in perspective taking by having them see their own environment through another person's eyes and to consider issues such as accessibility, fair distribution of resources, and discrimination in a very concrete way. With the intention of trying to make their neighborhood a comfortable place with a wide variety of people, children walk around in pairs, each child assigned to be a different "person" who imagines how that person would feel and what changes might make that person more comfortable. Possible roles are:

- a homeless person

- a very young child

- an elderly person

- a single parent with four children

- someone who speaks only French

- a member of a racial group not found in the neighborhood

- someone who cannot read

- someone who wants to grow his/her own vegetables

- a member of a family without a car

- a person in a wheelchair

- a blind person.

After children have walked around the neighborhood considering these people's potential experiences, they return to school and adjust their model to make the neighborhood a more accessible and comfortable place for a wider range of people. If they come up with some ingenious ideas, the teacher encourages them to write a letter with suggestions to the appropriate government officials.

Third Grade

Theme: Community Government

Activity: Visiting the City/Town Hall

This activity is often the culmination of a unit on city/town government and is designed to fulfill the following objectives:

1. to solidify children's understanding of the governing structure of their community by seeing the actual places where decisions are made;

2. to gain awareness of the actual people who do the governing;

3. to feel more comfortable in approaching elected and appointed officials.

The preparation for this field trip includes the following steps:

1. The teacher identifies particular officials children will meet and offices they will see.

2. The children prepare interview questions.

3. The teacher reviews local current events to see what issues are being discussed.

4. The children and teacher visit the city/town hall and tour the different offices.

5. They interview one or two officials.

6. Followup discussion occurs in the classroom.

Modifications

First, in preparation, children read the local newspapers and identify an issue that seems to be controversial and of interest to them—for example, a new housing development, the rezoning of a neighborhood, cutbacks in the school budget, the closing of a branch library, the construction of a highway that will cause some houses to be torn down.

Second, children learn as much as they can about the issue through reading the local newspapers, listening to the local news, and talking with their parents. If possible, the teacher can invite protagonists from all sides to visit the class and to discuss their positions with the children.

Third, children can try to understand the reasons for the conflicts of interest and see who benefits and who suffers by this change. For example, in the case of the housing development, they can follow the money trail to see who will make and who will lose money, whom the houses will be for (high-, middle-, or low-income families), and the gains and losses for the community as a whole (e.g., increased tax base versus loss of a potential park).

Fourth, children can debate the issue among themselves to clarify their individual stands and to gain skills in managing controversy.

Fifth, in their preparations for visiting the community government, they can prepare questions that relate to this issue and request interviews with the appropriate officials, preferably ones who can represent different points of view.

Sixth, in their discussions with city/town officials, children can learn more about the ways in which the decisions are made, the impact on local resources, plans to alleviate problems caused by this change, etc. If appropriate, they can present their ideas and arguments related to their issue.

Seventh, as part of the followup discussions, children who have strong opinions can write to the local newspaper and appropriate officials.

As these examples indicate, the subject matter of social studies can easily be adapted to meet the goals of multicultural education. Unfortunately, the traditional approaches have tended to narrow rather than broaden children's perspectives. By modifying the curriculum and shifting the overall perspective to be more expansive and inclusive, however, teachers can create a multicultural social studies curriculum.

REFERENCES

Damon, W. *Social and Personality Development.* New York: W. W. Norton, 1983.

Grant, Carl A., and Sleeter, Christine. *Turning on Learning: Five Approaches for Multicultural Teaching.* Columbus, Ohio: Merrill, 1989.

Jenness, Aylette. *Families: A Celebration of Diversity, Commitment and Love.* Boston: Houghton Mifflin, 1990.

Ramsey, Patricia G. "Beyond 'Ten Little Indians' and Turkeys: Alternative Approaches to Thanksgiving." *Young Children* (September 1979): 28–52.

_____ . *Teaching and Learning in a Diverse World: Multicultural Education for Young Children.* New York: Teachers College Press, 1987.

Chapter 3

INTEGRATING SCIENCE AND MATHEMATICS WITH A MULTICULTURAL PERSPECTIVE

by Meghan M. Twiest, Professor of Science Education, Indiana University of Pennsylvania

This chapter offers a historical picture of changing perspectives in science and mathematics in early childhood education. When juxtaposed with principles discussed in Chapter 1, it provides essential criteria to strengthen the process-oriented approach to teaching with a multicultural perspective. The sample lessons vary from contemporary science and mathematics content to lessons that are specifically designed with a multicultural perspective.

Only when I see males and females, Blacks, Hispanics, Native Americans, and Orientals having achievement in mathematics and science that is not affected by what sub-population they belong to will equity be achieved.

—Elizabeth Fennema 1984

INTRODUCTION

School reform reports of the 1980s have documented the failure of U.S. schools to teach science and mathematics. They describe the semiliteracy of many American children and adults in these fields. There is a demonstrated need to improve instruction in science and mathematics not only to regain our position in the international community but also to ensure a literate population able to take advantage of employment and career opportunities that require a solid scientific and mathematical foundation.

Specific recommendations from the many reports emphasize the need for prescribed courses prior to high school graduation (National Commission on Excellence in Education 1983) and emphasis on qualitative and logical reasoning (Business-Higher Education Forum 1983). Reports that specifically highlight curriculum and pedagogical changes include those of the Carnegie Forum (1986), the Twentieth Century Fund (1983), and the National Science Board Commission (1983). They state the need for new pedagogical approaches, a redefined and strengthened curriculum that includes designated science and mathematics sequences, and the incorporation of practical issues and the fostering of basic skills.

It is ironic that nearly 30 years earlier, another event significantly spurred public alarm and prompted federal spending to investigate the teaching of science and mathematics—the launching of the Soviet satellite Sputnik in 1957. Alarmed that the United States had slipped behind in the race to space, researchers and educators clamored for solutions—to improve the quality of science and mathematics education to enable the United States to regain its position as technological leader.

The findings after Sputnik revealed that science and mathematics were being poorly taught. Mathematics teaching relied heavily on rote memorization and computations; science relied almost entirely on reading from a text, answering questions at the end of the chapters, and completing definitions.

SCIENCE PROGRAMS 1960–90

In the 1960s and 1970s programs such as Elementary Science Study (ESS) (Education Development Center 1966), Science Curriculum Improvement Study (SCIS) (Berger, Karplus, and Montgomery 1969), and Science—A Process Approach (SAPA) (American Association for the Advancement of Science 1963) were developed and piloted. At the same time new mathematics curriculum programs such as the Comprehensive School Mathematics Program (CSMP) (CEMREL 1979) were also being developed. All these programs shared three basic premises: (1) they emphasized a hands-on learning approach; (2) they did not include a classroom textbook; and (3) they focused on the thinking or process skills, as well as the content to be learned. A few programs, specifically SAPA and the Minnesota Mathematics and Science Teaching Project (Minnemast) (1970), recognized the important relationship between science and mathematics and emphasized integration of the two areas.

Not until the 1980s was research available that compared students who were involved with these innovative programs with those who were not. This research showed that students involved in the programs had higher general achievement scores, higher science and mathematics scores, and better verbal fluency skills. By this time, however, enthusiasm for these programs had diminished. Federal funding for maintaining the programs had also disappeared.

Since then, innovative programs that integrate mathematics and science and that are developmentally appropriate for young children have become available. Two such programs are AIMS (Activities that Integrate Mathematics and Science) and GEMS (Great Explorations in Math and Science). Their activities encompass questioning, investigating, hypothesizing, and discovering; mathematics language provides the framework for understanding scientific concepts. Active learning, a hands-on approach, is a major component of both programs.

Along with the renewal of interest and the development of innovative science and mathematics education programs for the early years was a recognition of the fact that among those who were entering and succeeding in science and mathematics careers, certain groups, such as females and minorities, were underrepresented. For the most part, differences in science and mathematics achievement of females and minorities seem to be related to incongruence between teaching styles and learning styles, number of courses taken, access to quality facilities, and early tracking of racial and linguistic minorities who have had limited options for equality of instruction or equal access.

MULTICULTURAL CRITERIA FOR SCIENCE AND MATHEMATICS

The resurgence of multicultural education, the interest in making science and mathematics multicultural (National Science Teachers Association 1990; Woodrow 1984), and the statements on developmentally appropriate curriculum (Bredekamp 1987) have provided an impetus for examining the way we teach science and mathematics in early childhood classrooms. Combining the principles underlying multicultural education, what we know is developmentally appropriate for young children, and my own experiences teaching science education, I propose six criteria that are designed according to the process orientation described in Chapter 1.

First, consider the previous experiences of children in early childhood classes. If the children do not have a common experience, such as being able to look at a tree outside, it is necessary for the teacher to provide it. If the teacher assumes that most of the class has shared a common experience and teaches the lesson using the experience, those who have not had the experience will feel alienated, or unwilling or unable to participate. By giving all students a common experience, such as having an animal visit the classroom, taking a field trip to a zoo, or showing a video about zoo animals, teachers can ensure equal access to the concepts and experiences all children will need to further expand their knowledge.

Second, provide learning experiences that allow children to feel successful. Some teachers unknowingly expect children from minority and lower economic groups to fail. Often they are perceived as having fewer abilities and less potential (National Science Teachers Association 1990). In addition to poverty and prejudice in their daily lives, then, these children must face another institution that expects less of them. It is important that teachers of science and mathematics give all children experiences that encourage self-confidence. They can do this very easily, especially when individual class members manipulate materials on their own. For example, during a lesson using pennies, students observe how many drops of water will fit on a penny. As children proceed, they excitedly verbalize their accomplishments. Numbers continue to escalate as children try to get the most drops of water on their pennies. The teacher monitors students and joins in their excitement as pennies hold yet another drop. After the activity, the teacher asks several students not usually perceived as successful what their special secrets were for fitting so many drops of water on their pennies. Small episodes of success such as this can build confidence levels of all children, but especially of those for whom expectations of success were low.

Many children from underrepresented groups are excellent problem solvers, depending on the amount of independence they have been exposed to in their families and communities. This becomes apparent when students are involved in hands-on activities. Early childhood educators must capitalize on the problem-solving skills of these children—providing them opportunities to repair things, invent things, and manipulate equipment. As they use their strengths in problem-solving activities, they begin to see what is being taught as relevant to their personal lives and how their skills contribute to the success of others. Fear of failure and indifference to learning are absent from classrooms where all children have an opportunity to succeed.

Third, use content and materials that are developmentally appropriate. Most children in preschool and primary grades are either at the preoperational or concrete operational stage of development. Thus their materials in mathematics and science instruction should be concrete. As children become more mature, instruction materials gradually become more transitional and symbolic.

Fourth, provide role models in the classroom. Carl Grant (1977) proposed this criterion when he described staffing. Since a plurality of teachers in early childhood education are females, children need to have role models who love the challenges of science and mathematics. Too often female students learn from adult role models that it is feminine to be helpless in tasks that require problem-solving skills, such as repairing a leaky faucet or building a deck. With encouragement to work out problems on their own and nonsexist examples, female students see that they can be successful at any task.

In addition to exposing children from underrepresented groups to contributions of females, it is important to acquaint them with representatives from diverse racial groups who have made contributions in science and mathematics. Children should have an opportunity to interact with people who have used their knowledge and skills in science and mathematics to break through the mold of inequity. Journals such as *Discover, National Geographic,* and *Natural History* are good sources of current information about people in these fields. When possible, invite family or community members into the classroom to discuss their science- or mathematics-related careers, or how parents use science and mathematics skills in everyday life. Students may not choose their careers at this early age, but they must see that opportunities are open to them.

Fifth, as Williams described in Chapter 1, consider how children construct knowledge. I encourage teachers to integrate subject areas when possible to increase interest and incorporate the way children learn. Many students, including children of color, are more global than analytical in their approach to learning new concepts. Attempts to show relationships on a more global scale give these students a better chance for success. Mathematics and science share many common skills that are taught in grades K–3—for example, observing, communicating, graphing, measuring, estimating, and classifying. Preschool and primary teachers have found that the "thematic" or "unit" approach, which uses these skills with mathematics, language, and the arts, is an effective way to teach more in less time, to make learning relational and rational for a larger number of children.

Sixth, teach subject matter in ways that allow for use of discovery, problem solving, spatial visualization, and logical reasoning. Many children lack the ability to manipulate things in their minds, which puts them at a disadvantage. Giving them practice with this increases the efficiency with which they can grasp abstract concepts, and explore and develop their reasoning capabilities.

SAMPLE LESSONS

Following are sample lessons in science and mathematics that have a multicultural perspective. Though the six criteria listed above are not specific in each plan, they are embedded in the process. The more conventional science and mathematics lessons have been modified by use of enrichment activities—encouraging greater diversity in participation and more success.

Sample One: Types of Houses

Student learning activities will focus on the following concepts:

- identifying and distinguishing shapes of houses
- inferring why the shapes may differ
- designing houses with different shapes
- discovering the relationship between types of houses and the environment
- classifying houses according to shape.

Flash pictures of different houses on a large screen. Ask children to describe what they see. Then ask students to categorize what they have seen. Help students create a concept map of "house."

Discuss the different types of houses the children live in. Ask them to identify the shapes of their houses. Ask if they have ever seen houses shaped differently from theirs. Allow students to examine different types of houses from around the world and identify (a) the shape, (b) the material each is made of, and (c) the size (this can be identified as larger than, smaller than, or about the same as their house). As a class, have the children classify the houses according to shape. Have them make inferences as to why they are shaped differently.

To help children understand that the design of the house depends on the climate, the building materials available in the area, and the cultural background of the people, have them classify the houses by climate and materials used.

To extend the concept of house, have students make their own houses using paper towel tubes, shoe boxes, food containers, milk jugs, etc. They can create stories about their houses, including the materials used to make them, the type of climate the houses would be suitable for, and the types of families who might live in them.

Sample Two: A Celebration of Scientists and Mathematicians

Student learning activities will focus on the following concepts:

- appreciating contributions of scientists and mathematicians inclusive of minorities and women

- problem solving.

Ask students if they know the names of famous scientists or mathematicians. Some children may be familiar with such people as Thomas Edison, Benjamin Franklin, and Albert Einstein. If so, have them identify the important contributions of these men and discuss how life would be different if they had not invented things we use every day. Extend the discussion with examples of other famous scientists and mathematicians, who may not be as well known. Choose people from underrepresented groups such as the following:

- *George Washington Carver,* an African American, was an inventor. He developed 300 products from peanuts, 118 products from sweet potatoes, and 60 products from pecan nuts. Some of the products included bleach, shaving soap, paper, and ink.

- *An Wang,* an Asian American, is responsible for the original development of the basic components of digital computers. His invention is the principle upon which magnetic core memory is based. This resulted in the ability of computers to store information, which is the basic component of the modern computer.

Invite real scientists from the community from under-represented populations to talk about their jobs and some of the problems they have to solve. Extend the experience by providing biographies of Kegthug, a Native American; Ysidro M. Martinez, who invented the below-knee prosthesis (false leg); and Daniel Hale Williams, who performed the first open heart surgery in Chicago.

Inventors, who may be scientists or mathematicians, are problem solvers. They conduct experiments to try and solve those problems. Only after much trying and many failures do they solve the problem. Allow students to think about some problems they have in the classroom, such as finding out what the green stuff in the aquarium really is. Have students hypothesize about what they think could solve the problem. As a class, come up with a solution based on children's exploration of the problem.

Sample Three: Marine Animals

Student learning activities will focus on the following concepts:

- becoming familiar with various sea animals from around the world

- classifying and measuring animals according to length

- discovering how animals interact with their environment

- map interpretation.

During a unit on sea animals, seek out career women in marine science whose backgrounds differ from those of many of the children. They can share slides or show pictures of a variety of animals, from tiny starfish to larger animals such as dolphins and whales. If possible, bring to the classroom several small animals for the children to watch, touch, and interact with.

Continue the enrichment activities by taking the class outdoors where children can draw outlines (using chalk on the parking lot or string on the grass) of the actual sizes of the animals (using teacher-provided measurements). Have students label and discuss each of the lengths. Then have them determine the order of the animals from shortest to longest. The methods for making their comparisons may vary—for example, using string or lying down beside the measurements. Give children animal names and a picture of each so they can keep track of the sizes of the animals as they make comparisons. After returning to the classroom, check children's understanding by discussion rather than a written test.

The teacher can integrate further with reading and social studies. Children can read a story about the animals' natural habitats and then locate them on the map. Discuss such animals as sponges, shrimp, and sea turtles. Allow children to choose one of the animals studied to draw and create stories about its life in its natural environment. Encourage children to share their work. They may also discuss or write about the lives of children who live near bodies of water in the Pacific, the South, and other countries.

Sample Four: Tangrams

Student learning activities will focus on the following concepts:

- strengthening communication skills

- reinforcing the names of geometric shapes

- creating unique designs using two-dimensional shapes

34

- problem solving

- using inferences.

Give each child a set of tangrams—a Chinese puzzle consisting of two small triangles, one medium-sized triangle, two large triangles, a square, and a parallelogram. Allow time for children to explore with these materials. Use the tangram shapes to make a design on the overhead projector in the shape of a cat. Or ask a child to do this. Give children the opportunity to make the same design using their own set of tangrams. Encourage them to share where and how the shapes in the tangram puzzle appear in their home and community.

Pairing children indiscriminately allows for cross-communication and interaction with peers not always chosen. Placing a barrier between the partners so that they cannot see each other's tangram set allows children to work cooperatively to complete an exercise that requires one partner to make a design and then describe it to his/her partner so that he or she can reproduce the same design. Encourage children to describe placement of the figures using the names of shapes and other vocabulary words they feel will bring about a successful reproduction. Children learn quickly that everyone can communicate in spite of differences in language and dialect. They also develop skills in cooperative learning.

Sample Five: Exploring Outdoors

Student learning activities will focus on the following concepts:

- classifying natural objects

- counting five objects

- matching color

- observing and appreciating the environment.

Take a walk. Get as many parent volunteers as possible. One teacher enriched the activity by telling the children a story about a beautiful rainbow that shone, then crumbled to pieces and fell to the ground. She pulled out a small pouch with a rainbow embroidered on it, and told the children that on that day she gathered up the pieces and put them in the pouch. Then she gave each of the children a piece of the rainbow. Their task was to find five things in the area that matched the color of their rainbow chip (small tiles of various colors). The students were instructed to put small objects in the envelope provided and bring them back to the group for discussion. (To preserve nature, children can mark some objects with twist ties.)

Children can share the objects they found, observe all the objects that were found, and identify the most common and least common objects. They can also specify which colors were harder to find than others. The lesson can be enriched with a multicultural perspective when teachers allow children to select their favorite places to collect things. The diverse settings the children suggest, though far from the school setting, will influence the types of objects they will find and the level of interest of children who may think that decision making about where to explore is a task only for the teacher.

As these sample lessons illustrate, science and mathematics content can be modified to give the curriculum a multicultural perspective. With such lessons, children develop a more positive attitude toward mathematics and science. The end result, however, is more students who consider science and mathematics as a career option and a more educated populace.

CONCLUSION

This chapter has described ways to give all children the skills and ability necessary to succeed in science and mathematics using a multicultural perspective. The need to increase the success of minorities and females in all aspects of a growing, scientific, and technological society has been a major focus.

Successful science and mathematics experiences are the result of teaching and expanding concepts that have relevance and meaning in all children's lives.

REFERENCES

AIMS Education Foundation. *Project AIMS.* Fresno, Calif., 1987.

American Association for the Advancement of Science. *Science—A Process Approach: Commentary for Teachers.* Lexington, Mass.: Ginn, Xerox Education Division, 1963.

Berger, C.; Karplus, R.; and Montgomery, M. *Science Curriculum Improvement Study.* Berkeley: Lawrence Hall of Science, Regents of the University of California, 1969.

Bredekamp, Sue, ed. *Developmentally Appropriate Practice in Early Childhood Programs Serving Children from Birth Through Age Eight.* Washington, D.C.: National Association for the Education of Young Children, 1987.

Business-Higher Education Forum. "America's Competitive Challenge: The Need for a National Response." Washington, D.C., 1983.

Carnegie Forum. *A Nation Prepared: Teachers for the Twenty-First Century.* Report of the Carnegie Forum on Education and the Economy's Task Force on Teaching as a Profession. Washington, D.C., 1986.

CEMREL. *Comprehensive School Mathematics Program.* Final Experimental Version. St. Louis, Mo., 1979.

Education Development Center. *Elementary Science Study.* St. Louis: McGraw-Hill, Webster Division, 1966.

Fennema, Elizabeth. "A Dual Thrust in Mathematics and Science Education." Princeton, N.J.: CCSSO Leadership Institute, 1984.

Grant, Carl A. "Multicultural Education: Myth or Reality?" Unpublished paper. University of Wisconsin-Madison, 1977.

Great Explorations in Math and Science (GEMS) Project. Berkeley: Lawrence Hall of Science, Regents of the University of California, 1987.

Minnesota Mathematics and Science Teaching Project. Minneapolis: University of Minnesota, 1970.

National Commission on Excellence in Education. *A Nation at Risk: The Imperative for Reform.* Washington, D.C.: U.S. Government Printing Office, 1983.

National Science Board Commission on Precollege Education in Mathematics, Science, and Technology. *Educating Americans for the 21st Century.* 1983.

National Science Teachers Association. "Action Plan Outlines How to Improve the Education of Minority Students." *NSTA Reports,* March/April 1990.

Twentieth Century Fund. *Making the Grade.* New York, 1983.

Woodrow, Derek. "Cultural Impact on Children Learning Mathematics." *Mathematics in School,* November 1984.

Chapter 4

READING AND WRITING: A MULTICULTURAL PERSPECTIVE

by Edwina Battle Vold, Professor of Early Childhood Education, Indiana University of Pennsylvania

This chapter focuses on teacher characteristics that enhance the teaching of a curriculum with a multicultural perspective. Teachers in conventional and individualized classrooms create learning experiences for reading and writing that are both developmentally appropriate and culturally relevant. The sample lessons are from a variety of sources that deal with multicultural issues and how children can concomitantly develop reading and writing skills.

Reading and writing, like all human activities, can be seen as transactions in which individual and the social, cultural and natural elements reciprocally participate.
—Louise M. Rosenblatt 1989

INTRODUCTION

Teaching reading and writing through a multicultural perspective places the process and the content in a social/cultural context. Reading and writing are no longer simply skill acquisition (Murphy 1989), but processes through which cognition and understanding of self and others occur and where young children can begin to reconstruct the efficacy of the social and political systems they participate in. These systems include their classroom, families, and communities.

This chapter introduces the reader to two effective early childhood teachers at opposite poles who have used reading and writing as vehicles for social change. They are teachers who designed their curriculum in such a way that children learn to respect each other for what they are, to recognize the differences among them, and to realize that those differences make them unique persons. They learn that each of them can help make positive changes happen in their classrooms, homes, and neighborhoods (Hillman 1988). This chapter also contains seven activities in reading and writing with a multicultural perspective for kindergarten and primary grades.

TRADITIONAL CLASSROOM TEACHER

Ms. Sutton is an effective teacher of second graders in a small rural school. Like Pat Howard in *Lessons from a Child* (Calkins 1983), Ms. Sutton has a very structured classroom. She is a traditional teacher who uses her basal readers, gives spelling tests every Friday, uses her *Weekly Reader*s every Monday, and teaches social studies and science from the textbook, relying heavily on dittos to the exclusion of a hands-on approach. She teaches every subject separately. Her emphasis on a nontraditional approach to creative reading and writing combined with a multicultural perspective is the exception, however. She provides frequent experiences for children to discover that not all human experiences are the same, that similarities in values and traditions transcend cultural groups. Her students have many opportunities to logically think through real-life situations, to write about them, to read about real life by literary artists with different cultural and ethnic backgrounds. In fact, the one time in the week when Ms. Sutton's class is *not* quiet is when children are engaged during the Language Arts period. Like Pat Howard, Ms. Sutton is a lesson in contrasts, using teacher-directed and child-centered techniques, skills in context and skills in isolation (Calkins 1983).

Although I have wished the polarities in Ms. Sutton's class would disappear, I have found her commitment to multicultural education undaunted. Her participation in multicultural workshops and the resources found in her professional library have shaped much of what happens in her classroom. This new identity, however, is grounded in some past practices that required her to spend the month of September visiting with the families of each of the children in her classes to get to know their values, traditions, and behaviors. The impact of this practice of visitation and interaction with families and her new identification with the multicultural education movement are contributing factors to her success in using the social/cultural contexts and knowledge of development to make curriculum areas in reading and writing personally fulfilling to children.

INDIVIDUALIZED CLASSROOM TEACHER

In a culturally diverse classroom in a different school, I observed another teacher who is a genius in the classroom. His students fondly refer to him as Mr. J. Mr. J's classroom differed from Ms. Sutton's, showing more consistency in approach. It was child-centered and skill-oriented in all experiences. The sounds from children from diverse cultural groups revealed the many dialects and languages that typify communities inhabited by white ethnic groups, Pacific Islanders, urban African Americans, Asian groups, and Hispanics.

Reading and writing seemed to be occurring at all times, even when children were at work on mathematics problems or problem-solving activities in science and social studies. Oral storytelling and sharing of books (some in English, others with graphemic symbols unfamiliar to me but well worn from constant use) were frequent activities.

I observed a reading program that was individualized in design with traces of whole language interspersed throughout. Personalized and self-directed, the program allowed children to choose a wide variety of interesting and challenging books, textbooks, magazines, comic books, and community papers. As a part of the process, children were encouraged to write often. They wrote about their favorite book characters; they critiqued books and media. They wrote about themselves and others; they

41

graphed, recorded, and engaged in publishing and printing booklets and classroom newspapers.

Many children who did not speak English as a first language were engaged in cooperative learning with a peer and the teacher for partners. During their writing activities, they generally dictated experiences recorded by the teacher. Mr. J wrote their sentences in English to aid in translations and vocabulary building and to make the transition to bilingualism less difficult. He encouraged the children with varying dialects from Pidgin English to differing forms of Black English to express themselves freely in writing and in speech. He encouraged the dialectally different children to engage in editing some of the writing for publication to facilitate proficiency in the language of the school and to make the transition to becoming bidialectal a reality.

Although Mr. J's classroom was not identified as a multicultural education classroom, it met all the criteria:

1. The curriculum was appropriate, flexible, and unbiased, and it incorporated the contributions of all cultural groups.

2. It clearly based the affirmation of languages of cultural groups on difference rather than deficits.

3. The instructional materials were unbiased and nonstereotypical. A proliferation of books showed individuals from different cultural groups portraying different occupational and social roles (Grant 1978).

TEACHER CHARACTERISTICS

In both examples of classroom teaching styles, Ms. Sutton and Mr. J are the significant—if not the primary—factor in successfully incorporating a multicultural perspective in their curriculum. They purposefully design curriculum and experiences with a multicultural perspective and have certain characteristics in common. They are teachers who are

1. flexible in the way they plan activities

2. patient

3. cheerful and optimistic

4. independent and without the need to have complete control over other people and situations

5. intellectually curious and knowledgeable about diverse peoples and places

6. self-controlled, not easily upset

7. interested in children and their activities

8. accepting, respectful, and always affirming individual differences (Vold 1984).

Although all these characteristics are important, independence and intellectual security are highlighted since these two criteria are not found in the literature describing teachers for a multicultural classroom or in characteristics described in the chapters by Jalongo and Fennimore.

The independent teacher is secure and allows students to become independent. The independent teacher has no need to create environments in which children must adhere to the teacher's preconceived style, language behavior, or attitude. Children in such a classroom feel comfortable making choices and taking different routes to success.

The teacher who is intellectually secure is confident in her or his ability to teach all children. The secure teacher does not rely heavily on prescribed curricula with a monocultural perspective. Such a teacher knows the appropriate content and the processes needed to foster individual growth in academic areas and social skills. The intellectually secure teacher is able to detect deviations and gaps in children's development and to prescribe activities and materials to fulfill children's needs as they are revealed in individual conferences, more formal responses to classroom activities, sharing in large and small groups, and informal interactions between teacher and child (Vold 1984).

Some teachers find it difficult to be enthusiastic about incorporating a multicultural perspective in the curriculum. Neither Ms. Sutton nor Mr. J falls into this category. Both are cognizant of the positive outcomes of using a multicultural perspective in the classroom and the results of learning process skills such as reading and writing by doing. Through distinctly different styles of teaching, they have used reading and writing as process and content in helping children in very different classroom settings develop a knowledge and an understanding of the social/cultural context in which they live.

ACTIVITIES WITH A MULTICULTURAL PERSPECTIVE

Following are samples of activities that integrate reading and writing with a multicultural perspective. None of the activities is original. All have been designed, researched, and practiced in various classrooms. Some reflect a content approach, while others reflect a combination of content and process. References are provided for teachers who wish to expand their repertoire of lessons with a multicultural perspective.

I. All About Me

Use this activity at the beginning and end of the year. Encourage children to write their responses to the questions and discuss them in groups of four the following day during writing period.

Objective: The children identify in writing characteristics about themselves that can be shared with others orally.

Activity: What are two things I enjoy?
What are two things I don't enjoy?
What are two things I like to do alone?
What would I like to change about myself?

What person(s) do I admire most?
If I had one wish, what would I wish for? (Tiedt and Tiedt 1986)

II. What If . . . ?

Objective: To stimulate writing and to help children put in print their concerns regarding equity.

Activity: What if . . .
Everyone looked exactly the same?
I lived in the park on a park bench?
The woman sleeping on the grate invited me to dinner?
People were really the pets of animals? (Tiedt and Tiedt 1986)

For this activity, the teacher encourages children to write on Monday, share on Tuesday, and edit on Wednesday by reviewing punctuation and spelling. On Friday, some of the words used in their writings are included in a traditional spelling test.

III. The Oneness of All Human Beings

Objective: Children identify essential similarities with which we are born and those that we learn.

Activities: 1. Children read and discuss culturally oriented and developmentally appropriate literature in English or another language. For example,

Yashima, Taro. *Crow Boy.* New York: Viking Press, 1955.
This book tells the tale of a very small Japanese boy who, in the face of his classmates' scorn, finds his special way of learning.

Pogrebin, L. C., ed. *Stories for Free Children.* New York: Ms. Foundation for Education and Communication, 1982.

45

This anthology for elementary school children includes many stories written from a multicultural perspective.

Greenfield, E. *Africa Dream*. New York: John Day, 1977.

Written as a fantasy, this book is the account of a young girl's ideas of what it would be like to live in Africa. It could be used as a way of stimulating children's ideas of how people in other parts of the world live.

Yee, S., and Kokin, L. *Got Me a Story to Tell*. San Francisco: St. John's Educational Threshold Center, 1977.

With photographs and excerpts from taped interviews, children describe in their own words their experiences of living in this country. One story is about a child in a Black community; the others describe children's adjustments as they have moved from other places, including El Salvador, Hong Kong, the Fiji Islands, and the Philippines.

Tsow, M. *A Day with Ling*. London: Hamish Hamilton, 1982.

A visit to her Chinese classmate's house enables a child to experience the blend of English and Chinese traditions in various routines.

Maury, I. *My Mother and I Are Growing Strong*. Berkeley: New Seed Press, 1979.

This story of a Hispanic family shows how the mother and daughter learn that they have many abilities when they have to cope alone because the father is sent to prison.

These annotations and more can be found in Ramsey 1987.

2. Hold discussions about statements that are not supportive of equity, such as

- Let them speak English.
- Girls can't do things that boys do.
- My race is superior.

3. Have students make a list of characteristics people have in common. Bring in self-photos, talk, write about visible similarities to be read orally at children's developmental reading time (Pennsylvania Department of Education 1974).

IV. The Value of Cultural Pluralism to Society

Objective: Children learn to regard cultural and language pluralism in America as a mosaic rather than a melting pot.

Activities: 1. Have children write a play illustrating how languages borrow from one another.
2. Discuss how immigrants enrich any language.
3. Have children design bulletin boards to illustrate words in English borrowed from other languages (Tiedt and Tiedt 1986).

V. Group Identity and Value as Perceived by Others

Objective: Children delineate in their discussions and writing how language reflects the values of individuals and cultures.

Activities: 1. After reading literature, including newspapers and magazines in English and foreign languages, children critically analyze how self-image and impressions of others are affected positively and negatively.

2. Children write stories using local dialects and

47

jargon, expressing an understanding of their meanings without devaluing them. (This activity can be adapted to any environment for dialect speakers, including Pacific Islanders, African Americans, Native Americans, Asians, and others.

VI. Affirming Racial Physical Differences

Objective: Children are able to recognize and describe special characteristics of self and others emphasizing the wonderful mixture of differences.

Activities: 1. Make a book, "We All Look Special," by taking color photos of each child to be pasted on separate pages where children describe themselves in writing.

2. Read books about the beauty of black hair, such as *Cornrows* (Yarbrough 1979) and *Africa Dream* (Greenfield 1979). In a class with African-American children, support their pride in themselves and expand their awareness of diversity as well.

3. Children read, analyze, and write a critique of the book *People* by Peter Spier (1980).

VII. Folklore: Beliefs, Values, and Customs

Objective: Children learn to appreciate folklore of different ethnic and cultural groups and to increase their level of awareness of the types of folklore that exist.

Activities: 1. This lesson may be introduced by recalling the titles of folklore that children are familiar with and by identifying the ethnic/cultural groups that the stories are from.

2. Have children listen to the recording of a traditional Puerto Rican folktale, "Perez and

Martina," read by Pura Belpre (New York: CMS Records). Follow the first listening session by a discussion of the story including the characters, the plot, and the ending.

3. Discuss what it takes for a storyteller to make a story interesting. Replay the recording, asking children to listen very carefully for the techniques the storyteller used to make the listening enjoyable.

4. Make a list on chart paper of the various ways the storyteller uses the voice to tell the story (e.g., pitch, volume, and pace).

5. Have the class select one or two favorite folktales, myths, or legends; review the stories and, with the aid of a tape recorder, record one or two stories, involving several children in the retelling (Baker 1983).

These activities require the following resources: "Perez and Martina" (New York: CMS Records); "American Indian Stories from Children," vol. 1 (New York: CMS Records); "Hopi Tales" (New York: Folkways Records and Service Corporation).

CONCLUSION

As these activities reveal, developing skills in reading and writing with a multicultural perspective may also account for children's acquisition and construction of new knowledge about themselves and others and serve as a vehicle to consider issues related to equity. Children in the early childhood years need opportunities to examine their behaviors and attitudes with respect to the growing diversity of our population and the complexities inherent in maintaining a true democracy. Reading and writing as curriculum content and processes serve to bring these multicultural goals to fruition.

REFERENCES

Baker, Gwendolyn. *Planning and Organizing for Multicultural Instruction*. Reading, Mass.: Addison-Wesley, 1983. P. 155.

Calkins, Lucy McCormick. *Lessons from a Child: On the Teaching and Learning of Writing*. Portsmouth, N.H.: Heinemann, 1983.

_____. *The Writing Workshop: A World of Difference*. Portsmouth, N.H.: Heinemann, 1987.

Grant, Carl A. "Education That Is Multicultural—Isn't That What We Mean?" *Journal of Teacher Education* 29 (1978): 45–49.

Graves, Donald. *Writing: Teachers and Children at Work*. Exeter, N.H.: Heinemann, 1983.

Greenfield, E. *Africa Dream*. New York: John Day, 1979.

Hillman, Carol B. *Teaching Four-Year Olds: A Personal Journey*. Bloomington, Ind.: Phi Delta Kappa, 1988.

Mason, Jana, ed. *Reading and Writing Connections*. Boston: Allyn and Bacon, 1989.

Murphy, Sandra. "Establishing a Classroom Context for Reading and Writing Development." In *Reading and Writing Connections,* edited by Jana Mason. Boston: Allyn and Bacon, 1989.

Noyce, Ruth, and Christie, James. *Integrating Reading and Writing Instruction in Grades K–8*. Boston: Allyn and Bacon, 1989.

Pennsylvania Department of Education. *Equal Rights: An Intergroup Education Curriculum*. Harrisburg: Pennsylvania Department of Education, Office of Civil Rights, 1974.

Pflaum, Susanna W. *The Development of Language and Literacy in Young Children*. Columbus, Ohio: Merrill, 1986.

Ramsey, Patricia G. *Teaching and Learning in a Diverse World: Multicultural Education for Young Children*. New York: Teachers College Press, 1987.

Rosenblatt, Louise M. "Writing and Reading: The Transactional Theory." In *Reading and Writing Connections,* edited by Jana Mason, 154–55. Boston: Allyn and Bacon, 1989.

Spier, P. *People*. New York: Doubleday, 1980.

Tiedt, Pamela L., and Tiedt, Iris M. *Multicultural Teaching: A Handbook of Activities, Information and Resources.* Boston: Allyn and Bacon, 1986.

Tiedt, Sidney W., and Tiedt, Iris M. *Language Arts Activities.* Boston: Allyn and Bacon, 1987.

Vold, Edwina Battle. "Developing and Implementing an Individualized Program of Reading Instruction." In *Reading Instruction and the Beginning Teacher: A Practical Guide,* edited by James F. Baumann and Dale Johnson, 214–15. Minneapolis: Burgess, 1984.

Williams, Leslie R.; De Gaetano, Yvonne; Harrington, C. C.; and Sutherland, I. R. *ALERTA: A Multicultural, Bilingual Approach to Teaching Young Children.* Reading, Mass.: Addison-Wesley, 1985.

Yarbrough, C. *Cornrows.* New York: Coward-McCann, 1979.

Chapter 5

CHILDREN'S PLAY: A RESOURCE FOR MULTICULTURAL EDUCATION

by Mary Renck Jalongo, Professor of Early Childhood
Education, Indiana University of Pennsylvania

*In this chapter the author reveals how play supports
the goals of multicultural education. The teachers'
roles and responsibilities highlight how play becomes
a resource for multicultural education and for
effective teaching. The chapter contains typical
episodes of teacher/student behavior.*

Tell me what you play and I shall tell you who you are.
—R. Caillois 1961

How does the play of young children tell us who they are?
Although each child has a distinctive racial, cultural, ethnic,
socioeconomic, and individual identity, every child shares the
culture of childhood. A universal part of that childhood is
children's play. Consider how the play of these three preschool
children informs us about who they are:

Mohamad has recently immigrated to the United States from
his wartorn country. Observe his block play and you will see
the same scene repeated: replicas of people, animals,
vehicles, and buildings are scattered as he makes the sounds
of bombs exploding and anguished cries.

Jolene is a five-year-old in an urban Head Start classroom.
She bustles around the housekeeping area, answers the
incessant imaginary ring of a telephone, and turns down dates
with her insistent suitors. "No. I can't go out with you tonight."
She explains, "I have to take care of these kids. They always
make a mess . . . never clean up. I tell them 'clean up,' but they
never do."

Three-year-old Grant's favorite game is what he calls "Hide and Sneak," something he and his father invented one day while roughhousing together. Grant runs into his bedroom and conceals himself among several large stuffed toys. His father searches, pretending not to see him while Grant suppresses giggles. Through repetition, the game has been embellished. Now his father not only acts surprised at finding Grant but also treats him like a toy—giving him hugs, playfully dragging him around on the carpet, and tossing him onto the bed—all at Grant's suggestion and much to his delight.

These three play episodes not only tell us something about the lives of these children, but they also illustrate the three modern theoretical orientations to play: psychoanalytic, psychosocial, and constructivist (Isenberg and Quisenberry 1988).

In Mohamad's case, play seems to have a psychoanalytic purpose. He uses it to handle powerful emotions and gain control over frightening situations. In "playing out" situations that have made a great impression on them, children become masters of those situations (Freud 1920). From the psychoanalytic point of view, play serves a therapeutic function. In fact, play is so essential to mental health that the absence of playfulness in children is a sign of serious physical and emotional distress.

From the psychosocial perspective, play has not only inner emotional origins, but also a social purpose and context (Isenberg and Jalongo, in press). When Jolene refuses imaginary dates and complains about her imaginary children, she uses her play to express emotions and to "try on" social roles she has observed or imagines. As she interacts with other children who have different experiences, play expands her repertoire of social roles and contributes to her socioemotional growth.

When play is viewed from a Piagetian perspective, it is comparable to an adult's planning and problem-solving activity (Sutton-Smith 1988). Grant wants to prolong "Hide and Sneak," so he invents and reinvents the game. Through direct interaction with the people, objects, and events in his environment, Grant builds both his individual and his social competence (Inhelder 1969).

Dorothy Cohen (1972) summarizes the psychoanalytic, psychosocial, and cognitive-developmental values of play in this way: "Childhood play is a bulwark of mental health. Within its self-imposed structure, children set up and resolve challenges and conflicts that are physical, intellectual, and social in nature" (p. 337).

Clearly, play has value in children's lives. But how does it function as a resource for multicultural education?

MULTICULTURAL ASPECTS OF PLAY

Young children's play has eight essential characteristics (Fromberg 1987). It is voluntary, intrinsically motivated, symbolic, meaningful, active, pleasurable, rule-governed, and episodic. If we look at the influences of the child's culture on each characteristic, we begin to appreciate how play supports the goals of multicultural education.

Play is voluntary and intrinsically motivated by such things as inquisitiveness, competence motivation, the need for social acceptance, and so forth. For example, Tatiana, a three-year-old Russian child, received a set of "Matryoshka," wooden nesting dolls in brightly painted traditional costumes, that had belonged to her grandmother and her mother. The toy quickly became her favorite. Tatiana was motivated to play with the toy because it intrigued her, because she eventually mastered its sequence, and because it became social reinforcement as a marker of her intergenerational connections.

Play is symbolic and meaningful. It represents reality with an "as if" or "what if" attitude and connects or relates experience with those representations of reality. Those symbols and the values attributed to them are a reflection of the child's culture (Vold 1985). For example, Ms. DeLorenzo changes the materials in the restaurant/cooking corner of her classroom weekly to reflect the symbols of different cultures. One week, she equips the center with an electric wok, rice bowls, a teapot, and an audiocassette of authentic Chinese music. She also includes chopsticks and the menu from a Chinese restaurant owned by the family of one of her students. The children follow a rebus recipe for a simple stir fry and play throughout the week with the props provided. For some children, the meaning of these symbols is reassuringly familiar; for other children, the symbols are new ways of learning about others.

Play is active and pleasurable. Children are participants who are enjoying themselves, even if they are serious about the activity. The social context will affect the child's selection of activities and the level of satisfaction derived from the play.

Consider, for example, a historical account of children's play on the American frontier (West 1989). In the mid-1800s, children in an Arizona mining camp invented a nighttime game called "All the Tigers Are Gone."

> One child, the tiger, would slip away among trees and boulders. The rest remained at home base for a time, then dispersed into the dark, calling occasionally, "All the tigers are gone." Guided by these shouts, the tiger would stalk and pounce and anyone caught became in turn a tiger who began prowling for victims. There was a delicious tension here for no one wanted to be among the first caught, yet to be the last, creeping among the deep shadows, enemies all around, was even less enviable. (West 1989, 113).

Notice how the children's spontaneous play prepared them for the dangers they feared most: getting lost and being attacked by a wild animal. The game illustrates an important paradox about play, namely, that it is fun and serious at the same time.

Play is rule-governed. The social mores of the group will determine what is acceptable behavior. Sometimes those rules are implicit; at other times the rules are made explicit, as in this exchange between two preschool girls:

Anna: You be the baby and I'll be the mommy.

Shelley:	Can I have some candy?
Anna:	OK, as much as you want.
Shelley:	But, Anna, you are the *mommy*. You have to give me *what's good for me.*
Anna:	I know. You can have a lot.

When children encounter rules that are different from the ones they have experienced, it causes them to wonder and raises their level of awareness. Introduction, awareness, and consciousness-raising are, in fact, a recommended starting point for multicultural education (Gay 1979). These attitudes are a first step in breaking down the barriers of prejudice.

Play is episodic. Children's roles and goals change and develop, based upon their experiences in society. When teachers share captivating stories with children and invite them to enact those stories, the dramatization often carries over into their play. Teachers can make even abstract ideas such as social inequity concrete for the young child through the dramatization of nonfiction books such as *Follow the Drinking Gourd* (Winter 1988) or fictional stories such as *Claude the Dog: A Christmas Story* (Gackenbach 1974).

TEACHERS' ROLES AND RESPONSIBILITIES

Play is a tremendous resource for bringing a multicultural perspective to an early childhood program because it "enables children to grow out of their egocentric and ethnocentric picture of the world" (Kendall 1983, 10). Realizing play's potential for multicultural education basically involves six things:

1. Be aware that multiculturalism "must begin with the adults" (Casanova 1987).

Multicultural education is first and foremost attitudinal. To function in a culturally pluralistic society, adults need to have a commitment to all the cultural groups in which they participate, they must function in more than one culture simultaneously, and they must be able to examine their own culture from an outsider's perspective (Ramirez 1983). By modeling these attitudes, we build children's self-esteem, give children a sense of their heritage, and promote intercultural understanding.

Ms. Ochoa teaches kindergarten in an economically depressed area where many of the children live in trailer courts. She overhears two children who are building a house with blocks as they discuss their concept of a habitat:

Bradley: No, you can't live in a trailer, you've got to live in a house.

Carol Ann: But I do live in a trailer.

Bradley: A trailer is for camping. You've gotta live in a house or maybe an apartment.

Ms. Ochoa could ignore the children's dilemma, leaving Carol Ann with the feeling that her home was something to be ashamed of. In this case, she would come away from school with the same feelings of inferiority that Native American Joseph Suina (1987) described:

The winter months are among my fondest recollection. A warm fire crackled and danced brightly in the fireplace and the aroma of delicious stew filled our one-room house. To me the house was just right. The thick adobe wall wrapped around us protectingly during the long, freezing nights. Grandmother's affection completed the warmth and security I will always remember. . . . And then I came to school . . . the classroom . . . was terribly huge and smelled of medicine like the village clinic I feared so much. The walls and ceiling were too far from me and I felt naked. The fluorescent light tubes were eerie and blinked suspiciously above me. . . . The English language and the new set of values caused me much anxiety and embarrassment. . . . The Dick and Jane reading series in the primary grades presented me pictures of a home with a pitched roof, straight walls and side walls. . . . It was clear that I didn't have these things and what I did have didn't measure up. At night, long after grandmother went to sleep, I would lay awake staring at our crooked adobe walls casting uneven shadows from the light of the fireplace . . . my life was no longer just right, I was ashamed of being who I was and I wanted to change right then and there. (p. 392)

Instead of underscoring the message that living in trailers or adobe or apartments or condos is something to be ashamed of, Ms. Ochoa initiates a "Where do they live?" bulletin board/ collage. Her pictures come from old magazines such as *National Geographic, Life,* and *Old House Journal.* She also finds that UNICEF has a set of notecards called "International Neighbors" and calendars that contain both photographs and children's drawings of homes from around the world. The children use the materials as resources and create their own to develop an impressive display of different habitats. As a result of Ms. Ochoa's efforts, every child's concept of what a home can be or look like is extended.

2. Know your students and their cultural backgrounds (West 1986).

Robin is a four-year-old girl who is a full-blooded Sioux. Her favorite game is "Pow," short for powwow. During the summer, Robin participated in many of these gatherings with other groups of Native Americans representing tribes from all over the United States. Usually a powwow lasts for two or three days and includes such activities as dancing, storytelling, selling wares, and judging costumes. When Robin plays Pow, she takes her daughter (a Native American doll) to see the events. Her father plays the roles of merchant, dancer, and storyteller.

To illustrate how knowledge of children's cultural backgrounds can enrich the curriculum, we need only compare/ contrast Robin's spontaneous behavior with a "lesson" on Native

Americans in a kindergarten in the same community. The children make paper bag fringed "vests" and construction paper feather headbands, and have a "powwow" by sitting in a circle and singing "Ten Little Indians." If you asked any of these children whether Indians are alive today, they would surely say no. Furthermore, these children have the mistaken notion that a powwow is an uneventful circle time activity. Next year when Robin is in that class, she can enrich the children's and the teacher's understandings about Native American traditions. Perhaps the teacher could relate a powwow to an event that is both important and familiar to these rural children's lives: the county fair. But none of this can happen unless the teacher gets to know Robin and helps her feel comfortable about bringing play themes from her racial and ethnic background into the classroom.

3. Expect conflict and model conflict resolution.

We cannot expect a classroom spirit of one big happy family to occur automatically, any more than we can expect children with similar cultural backgrounds to share toys without modeling and positive reinforcement.

Six-year-olds Brooke and Johnny reveal conflicting ideas about sex roles and parental responsibility.

Brooke: Hey, Mandy! Let's play house. Johnny, you're the daddy and I'm the mommy. Mandy's the baby.

Johnny: Why can't I be the baby today? I'm always the daddy.

Brooke: Because you're a boy. Girls can't be daddies.

Mandy: Ga-ga, goo-goo. Me want milk.

Brooke: Here's your bottle, Mandy.

Mandy: Yum, yum, drink it all up now.

Johnny: Let's put baby Mandy to bed now and we'll go

grocery shopping.

Brooke: OK. (Brooke throws a small blanket over Mandy, who is lying down, and she and Johnny leave.) We can't be there too long because Mandy might get awake.

Johnny: We don't need too much stuff.

Brooke: I'll take coupons and you take money. We need milk, eggs, pancakes, and cookies. (Brooke and Johnny walk to the adjacent area of the room, the grocery store.)

Johnny: We have to go now.

Brooke: You carry this stuff. You're the daddy. (They reenter the housekeeping area. Mandy is awake and crawls on the floor toward them.) Look, we should've left before! Mandy might have got hurt. Next time, you go to the store by yourself.

Johnny: I don't want to play with you anymore. I'm leaving.

Brooke: Well, I don't care. Me and Mandy will be mommy and baby then. We don't need daddy. My daddy's never home, so there.

The teacher uses her observations of this play episode to shape the curriculum. Rather than the tired old "All About Me" individual booklet, Ms. Hatlani decides to create group big books entitled *What Is a Mother?* and *What Is a Father?* She begins by instructing her first graders to observe the mothers and fathers they see during the week and to write or draw a list of some of the things that parents do for children. They write a list of their findings on the board, and then organize their ideas on chart paper. Pairs of children select a page to write and illustrate. They discuss their ideas; they do a rough draft of the writing, drawing, and arrangement on newsprint; then they make the final copy on poster-sized paper with markers. The finished products are bound and put on display for open house. The activity has not only broadened children's views of parental responsibilities, but it has also encouraged cooperation between and among the class members.

4. Bring the outside world into the classroom and help parents see the value of play firsthand.

Jacobs (1987) describes a project in Israeli kindergartens in which parents were invited to talk about the country where they were born, stressing memories and facts that would interest a young child. This same approach could be used to support children's play. Parents might be asked to bring a toy and/or photographs that are artifacts from the play of their own childhoods, to describe some favorite play themes and activities, and to explain why that play was so memorable and enjoyable. A good picture book to introduce this theme is Pomerantz's *The Chalk Doll* (1989), in which a mother describes her poverty during childhood and her longing for a real doll. By sharing toys from their own childhoods, community members are reminded of the importance of play in children's lives and become more supportive of play in the classroom. Interacting with adults about their play can enhance children's imaginations and intercultural awareness.

5. Present modern concepts of families and occupations.

Four-year-old Crystal lives with her mother, her maternal grandfather, her aunt, and her two-year-old cousin in Detroit. When Crystal plays Cops and Robbers, she encounters some sex role stereotypes that are completely foreign to her; Jerrell insists that "only big, strong men" can be police officers and that he can escape because she is "just a girl." Mrs. Potter, Crystal's teacher, realizes that simply telling Jerrell that he is incorrect is unlikely to have much effect. When teaching young children, social rules are not *covered*, they are *discovered* through specific contexts and real-life situations (Hall 1984). Mrs. Potter speaks with Crystal about bringing someone special to their group discussion time. Before that person arrives, Mrs. Potter begins with two questions: "Who can be a police officer?" and "Why?" Most children have the impression that men are police officers "because they're strong," or "because they have to catch the bad guys." Then Crystal's mother arrives in full police officer's uniform and greets the children. They even go out onto the playground and look at her patrol car and she responds to their questions. When one child asks, "Is your daddy a policeman too?" Crystal's nonstereotypic family structure is also explained as Mrs. Potter looks on approvingly. Now when Crystal wants to play police officer, no one doubts her ability to play the role authoritatively.

6. Use literature to enrich children's play and understandings about cultural pluralism.

Literature contributes to children's play because it

- communicates the universality of human emotions, as in *My Friend* (Gomi 1990) or *This Is the Way We Go to School: A Book About Children Around the World* (Baer 1990).

- models prosocial behavior, as in *Chita's Christmas Tree* (Howard 1990) and *Oma and Bobo* (Schwartz 1989).

- gives children pride in their ethnic heritage, as in *Mufaro's Beautiful Daughters* (Steptoe 1987) and *Thunder Cake* (Polacco 1990).

- introduces children to contemporary families both alike and different from their own, as in *A Chair for My Mother* (Williams 1982) and *How My Parents Learned to Eat* (Friedman 1984).

- reveals to children how it feels to be different, as in *I Hate English!* (Levine 1990) and *The Black Snowman* (Mendez 1990).

- enables children to participate in another social era, as in *The King's Day: Louis the IX of France* (Aliki 1989) or *The Boy of the Three Year Nap* (Snyder 1988).

- shows a wide range of human characteristics and aspirations, as in *Knots on a Counting Rope* (Martin and Archambault 1987), *Laura Charlotte* (Galbraith 1990), or *Nessa's Fish* (Luenn 1990).

- immerses children in another culture or subculture's folklore, as in *The Talking Eggs: A Folktale from the American South* (San Souci 1989) or the East African tale *How the Guinea Hen Got Her Spots* (Knutson 1990).

CONCLUSION

As Williams (1989) observes:

"Culture" consists of all the people, objects and events that impart meaning to our lives. It is not only our past history and traditions observed in our families, but also the detail of our present, everyday lives. Cultures change from generation to generation, from locale to locale. Still, there is a thread of connection that allows us to belong to one or more groups and to derive at least a part of our identity from that belonging. Young children share in that connection. (p. 3)

Play is an integral part of that connectedness. It is the tie that binds together the culture of childhood, a rich resource for curricula and programs with a multicultural perspective, a link between and among social groups, and, perhaps most importantly, a clear message about who children are.

REFERENCES

Casanova, U. "Ethnic and Cultural Differences." In *Educator's Handbook: A Research Perspective,* edited by V. Richardson-Koehler, 379–92. New York: Longman, 1987.

Cohen, D. *The Learning Child.* New York: Pantheon/Random House, 1972.

Freud, S. *Beyond the Pleasure Principle.* London: Hogarth Press, 1920.

Fromberg, D. P. "Play." In *The Early Childhood Curriculum: A Review of Current Research,* edited by C. Seefeldt, 35–74. New York: Teachers College Press, 1987.

Gay, G. "On Behalf of Children: A Curriculum Design for Multicultural Education in the Elementary School." *Journal of Negro Education* 48 (1979): 324–40.

Hall, E. *Beyond Culture: The Dance of Life.* Garden City, N.Y.: Doubleday, 1984.

Inhelder, B. *The Psychology of the Child.* New York: Basic Books, 1969.

Isenberg, J., and Jalongo, M. R. *Creative Expression and Play in Early Childhood Education.* New York: Macmillan, in press.

Isenberg, J., and Quisenberry, N. "Play: A Necessity for All Children." *Childhood Education* 64, no. 3 (1988): 138–45.

Jacobs, R. "Cultural Differences: Clarification for Young Children. *Early Child Development and Care* 28 (1987): 163–65.

Kendall, F. E. *Diversity in the Classroom: A Multicultural Approach to the Education of Young Children.* New York: Teachers College Press, 1983.

Laughlin, C., and Suina, J. "Reflecting the Child's Community in the Classroom Environment." *Childhood Education* 60, no.1 (1983): 19–21.

Ramirez, M. *Psychology of the Americas: Mestizo Perspectives on Personality and Mental Health.* New York: Academic, 1983.

Ramsey, P. G.; Vold, E. B.; and Williams, L. R. *Multicultural Education: A Source Book.* New York: Garland, 1989.

Suina, J. H. Quoted in Casanova, U. "Ethnic and Cultural Differences." In *Educator's Handbook: A Research Perspective,* edited by V. Richardson-Koehler, 379–92. New York: Longman, 1987.

Sutton-Smith, B. "Children's Play." In *Leaders in Education: Their Views on Constructive Issues,* edited by G. F. Roberson and M. A. Johnson, 165–67. Lanham, Md.: University Press of America, 1988.

Swick, K. J. *Readings on Multicultural Learning in Early Childhood Education.* Little Rock, Ark.: Southern Association of Children Under Six, 1987.

Vold, E. B. "Understanding America and Its Peoples." *Dimensions* 13, no. 4 (1985): 4–6.

Wardle, F. "Are You Sensitive to Interracial Children's Special Identity Needs?" *Young Children* 42, no. 2 (1987): 53–59.

West, B. "Culture Before Ethnicity." *Childhood Education* 62, no. 3 (1986): 175–81.

West, E. *Growing Up with the Country: Childhood on the Far Western Frontier.* Albuquerque, N.M.: University of New Mexico Press, 1989.

Williams, L. R. "Diverse Gifts: Multicultural Education in the Kindergarten." *Childhood Education* 66 (1989): 2–3.

CHILDREN'S BOOKS

Aliki. *The King's Day: Louis the IX of France.* New York: Crowell, 1989.

Baer, F. *This Is the Way We Go to School: A Book About Children Around the World.* New York: Scholastic, 1990.

Friedman, I. R. *How My Parents Learned to Eat.* Boston: Houghton Mifflin, 1984.

Gackenbach, D. *Claude the Dog: A Christmas Story.* New York: Scholastic, 1974.

Galbraith, K. O. *Laura Charlotte.* New York: Putnam/Philomel, 1990.

Gomi, T. *My Friend.* New York: Chronicle Press, 1990.

Howard, E. F. *Chita's Christmas Tree.* New York: Bradbury, 1990.

Knutson, B. *How the Guinea Hen Got Her Spots.* New York: Carolrhoda, 1990.

Levine, E. *I Hate English!* New York: Scholastic, 1990.

Luenn, N. *Nessa's Fish.* New York: Atheneum, 1990.

Martin, B., and Archambault, J. *Knots on a Counting Rope.* New York: Holt, 1987.

Mendez, P. *The Black Snowman.* New York: Scholastic, 1990.

Polacco, P. *Thunder Cake.* New York: Putnam/Philomel, 1990.

Pomerantz, C. *The Chalk Doll*. New York: Lippincott, 1989.

San Souci, R. D. *The Talking Eggs: A Folktale from the American South.* New York: Dial, 1989.

Schwartz, A. *Oma and Bobo*. New York: Bradbury, 1989.

Snyder, D. *The Boy of the Three Year Nap*. Boston: Houghton Mifflin, 1988.

Steptoe, J. *Mufaro's Beautiful Daughters*. New York: Lothrop Lee and Shepard, 1987.

Williams, V. *A Chair for My Mother*. New York: Greenwillow, 1982.

Winter, J. *Follow the Drinking Gourd*. New York: Knopf, 1988.

Chapter 6

THE MULTICULTURAL CLASSROOM CLIMATE

by Beatrice S. Fennimore, Professor of Early Childhood Education, Indiana University of Pennsylvania

This chapter extends the multicultural perspective beyond the subject areas in the classroom. It examines real issues that evolve in classroom interactions that can best support a multicultural curriculum. The AVIMA model is a conceptual guideline for use by all teachers.

Everything the teacher does, as well as the manner in which he does it, incites the child to respond in some way or another and each response tends to set the child's attitude in some way or another.

—John Dewey 1933

CLASSROOM LIFE BETWEEN THE LINES

Classroom life is composed of a complex set of social relationships that impact daily on the sense of acceptance and self-esteem of each child. Every child brings to those relationships the "baggage" of experience, home life, race, culture, and individual personality. In every classroom the teacher is the critical variable in the translation of children's personal qualities and experiential realities into a whole classroom environment that welcomes, values, and encourages each child. The goals of multicultural education are therefore relevant to each personal decision affecting relationships that teachers make every day (Ramsey 1987).

Somewhere between the lines—even the lines of relatively equal exposure to the same quality of educational experience—schools that focus on dominant culture and style can somehow convince children outside that dominant culture and style that they lack the gifts and merits necessary for success (Bordieu and Passeron 1977). This chapter focuses on the possible opposite effect of a "between-the-lines" multicultural classroom climate that directly addresses the presence of diversity with an observably positive and productive attitude.

MULTICULTURAL CLASSROOM CLIMATE

What is the classroom climate? Oakes (1985) describes classroom climate as the relationships between all classroom participants, the quality of goal orientation toward personal development, and the maintenance of a classroom organizational system. Personal and interpersonal "feelings" are critical to the psychological forces that influence the social environment of groups and subgroups in classrooms. This chapter defines the multicultural classroom climate as the fully established atmosphere that can be observed to reflect and respect racial, cultural, gender, ability, and age diversity (Boyer 1985) through classroom design, use of curriculum, and personal interaction between teacher and child. The multicultural personal interaction between teacher and child can be observed in arrival and departure greetings and behaviors, transitional activities during the school day, the teacher's mannerisms when calling on and responding to children during class time, and the teacher's manner of verbal discipline while teaching lessons.

OVERLYING MULTICULTURAL CONCEPTS

What overlying concepts can be used to evaluate observed teacher behaviors that determine the multicultural classroom climate? A dedication to equity for all children, a knowledge of the critical impact of teacher expectation on student achievement, and a determination to be an advocate for all children, all serve as critical guidelines. Equity is defined as the equal opportunity for all children to be exposed to excellence in education and to reach their highest potential (Smith 1989). Teacher expectation describes the link between teacher beliefs about student abilities and the impact of those beliefs on ultimate student achievement outcomes. Advocacy is defined as a personal commitment to active involvement in the lives of children beyond remunerated professional responsibilities with the goal of enhancing the opportunities of all children for optimal personal growth and development (Fennimore 1989). Teachers guided by these three concepts will be able to implement a multicultural classroom model for children.

A MULTICULTURAL CLASSROOM MODEL FOR TEACHERS

What model might teachers use to ensure that the climate of their classroom is observably multicultural? The AVIMA model (Fennimore 1991) provides a conceptual guideline enabling teachers to analyze and focus their attitudes and subsequent classroom and social behavior. The AVIMA model follows these steps:

- Teachers ACCEPT the diversities in their classroom in a nondeficit approach to the realities of children.

- Teachers VALUE the diversities as a challenge to the successful preparation of all children for life in a multicultural world, and are determined to find the valuable skills and attributes of all children.

- Teachers IDENTIFY and articulate exactly what they can accomplish for their students regardless of diversities (such as learning disabilities, unemployed parents, or family abuse situations) that might be perceived as discouraging negatives.

- Teachers willingly MODEL excellence, acting as school leaders in terms of their positive and productive approach to diversity.

- Teachers ADVOCATE for children through design of classroom interaction, professional peer interaction, and social interaction that might impact on the acceptance and positive valuing of their students.

BALANCING THE REAL AND THE IDEAL

The acceptance of multicultural diversity in modern society suggests a well-developed understanding of human differences, and at times the placement of potentially negative facts about children or their families in a context of positive determination to have faith in the ultimate potential and possibility of every child. One in five children in America is poor, one in six children has no health insurance, one in seven is at risk for dropping out of school, and one of two children has a mother in the labor force in a society that offers inadequate day care for its minorities (Edelman 1989). Natriello, McDill, and Pallas (1989) have identified five key indicators associated with children who are educationally disadvantaged: (1) different race or ethnicity, (2) poverty, (3) single-parent families, (4) poorly educated mothers, and (5) limited English proficiency.

Teachers determined to create a multicultural classroom climate understand that not all children with these indicators are educationally disadvantaged. They will be on guard against any possibility that they increase disadvantage in their own class-rooms because of negative or stereotypical assumptions about children. No matter what the realities may be, an outside observer should form a strong impression that all members of the class are accepted and supported through room decoration, curriculum materials, and personal interaction between teacher and child. Teachers can accomplish this with a sense of advocacy, a commitment to human equity, and a dedication to high expectation for all children.

Room Decoration and
Multicultural Classroom Climate

The multicultural classroom reflects the lives and interests of those within, but it also encourages knowledge and respect for all the people of the world. Teachers should give careful thought to commercial room decorations to determine if they do or do not incorporate all the races, cultures, and personal realities of the children. In addition, all classrooms (racially or culturally homogeneous as well as heterogeneous) should expose children to visual reminders of diversity. Throughout their careers, teachers can maintain files of multicultural pictures from magazines, newspapers, and other sources to supplement materials available in the school. It is important to display such pictures of people of many colors, of different forms of housing, of geographic settings from rural to urban, and of different expressions of cultural events and holidays, and to discuss these topics formally and informally throughout the school year.

Added to room decorations should be bulletin boards and other displays that contain photographs of the children in the classroom. Perhaps parents can supply them, or the school may provide a camera for the teacher to use. Commercial school photographs may be available, or children may draw pictures of themselves and their families. Children may also supply pictures of pets, families, homes, or other areas of interest. Experience charts, essays, or other writing activities that reflect on personal experiences, thoughts, and feelings add to the positive tone of a classroom decorated in a multicultural style. The use of photographs and written work to create positive peer relationships and cooperative learning further indicates that students are encouraged to accept each other as friends and equals.

Multicultural Curriculum Materials

Most teachers are under some obligation to use certain materials and teach the curriculum that their programs or school districts require. But there are still many choices available to teachers who want to instill a multicultural classroom climate. If textbooks fail to incorporate information about and coauthored by individuals from certain groups, teachers can take steps to make students aware of diverse contributions through discussion and classroom displays. Public library books chosen on the basis of positive reflection of diversity (as well as the problems diversity sometimes poses to children) can be available in the classroom for weekly or monthly use. Learning centers and other teacher-created learning materials can teach required curriculum while still providing the opportunity for expansive thought on different people and places.

The teacher who is multiculturally aware can almost never be text and worksheet bound. It is essential to supplement commercially prepared written curriculum materials with exposure to music, art, artifacts, and structured activities that allow freedom for exploration and cooperative learning. Certainly, such supplementation requires hours of research, study, and preparation of materials and activities throughout the year, but in all likelihood expanding the basic curriculum in a multicultural direction will make teaching a more rewarding and exciting occupation. Larry Cuban (1970) suggests that teachers work creatively to add four components to the classroom curriculum: (1) people-centered materials; (2) concrete materials; (3) materials that allow children to discuss and reflect on the problems, possible conflicts, and formation of choice and opinion created by human diversity in its many forms; and (4) materials that are relevant in terms of student experiences, learning styles, and individual strengths and weaknesses. The school-based curriculum is only a departure point for the teacher committed to multicultural curriculum.

Multicultural Interpersonal Interaction

Even more important than curriculum and room design are the tone and quality of interpersonal relationships in the classroom. Teachers can sometimes be surprised to learn that an outside observer can quickly identify students considered by teachers to be behavior problems, or slow learners, or less interested in school success. This is possible because the teachers have altered their behavior and tone of interaction with these students, and this can be obvious even when there is no discernible problem in the classroom observation. How can teachers avoid such reactions? They can focus on equitable and positive classroom behaviors at arrival and departure time, during lesson transitions, when calling on and responding to different students during lessons, and in the manner and tone of their verbal classroom discipline. These teacher behaviors should exhibit equity in spite of test scores, assigned tracks, labels applied to individual children, or negative information about family or community. Such equitable behaviors would indicate that there is no sense of permanency in decisions about the ultimate potential of children (Fennimore 1989). The objective observer in a classroom with a multicultural climate would see equal opportunities for every child to be engaged, to experience success, to be encouraged, and to receive limitless opportunities to improve behavior and classroom performance.

Arrival and Departure of Students

Teachers who want to establish a multicultural classroom environment consciously and thoughtfully design ways of greeting and saying farewell to their students each day. The greeting indicates "This is a new day! I think you can be a tremendous success today." It should be extended to each child as he or she enters the room or the school. The departure should communicate "No matter what happened today, I am still your teacher and tomorrow is a new day in every way." A smile, a touch, and eye contact make a big difference to children. A sense of welcome and comfort at the start of the day and a sense of accomplishment and satisfaction at the end of the day will make school a more accepting and comfortable place for all children.

Is it really possible for teachers to feel and act in such a positive way when children can be difficult and when realities of

73

classroom life can be so challenging? Yes, as long as teachers remember that they have dedicated themselves to optimal development for all children in their care. Even adults often act in difficult ways that others must overlook to retain positive relationships. Children who are in rapidly changing stages of developmental growth must know that they have a continuous opportunity to meet the expectations of their classroom teachers.

Classroom Transitions

Children move from lesson to lesson, from floor to desk, from gym to science lab, from reading lesson to lavatory—generally experiencing regular transit throughout the day. The appropriate teacher tone during transitions is one of congratulation, encouragement, empathy, or understanding. Transitions provide an opportunity for brief student-enhancing interactions. Teachers can focus on student achievements and remind students of how well they are doing. They can say, "All right, class 102, greatest class in the school, let's see if we can finish and be back in our seats by one o'clock!" or "I know we're tired, but we can do it!" Teachers in a multicultural classroom climate want to avoid stern and unsmiling directions, unnecessary rigidity (Must students always be silent, or in single file?), and obvious antagonisms ("All right, James. I'm watching you. No trouble from you. Get in your seat and stay there. Now."). There should be no difference in quality and tone of school transitions between schools in more or less advantaged neighborhoods—the same positive and warm tone of personal interaction during transitions is possible in all schools.

Calling On and Responding To Children

Some children seem to spend the entire day raising their hands, and some almost never respond to questions. Every classroom, whatever label it may have (i.e., "gifted," "learning disabled," "normal"), has a heterogeneous mix of individual abilities. The classroom with a multicultural climate must provide daily opportunities for all children to be engaged in a

74

positive way. Teachers can design activities in ways that ensure equal engagement of all students. They can show consistency in the way they call on and respond to children—meeting every answer with a nod or a smile and positive reinforcement of some kind. Even when answers are incorrect, teachers can reinforce the attempt, try to explain the error, and return to the student later in the lesson to provide an opportunity for success. They can also provide every student with equitable prompting, wait time, and encouragement.

One helpful technique is to make a checklist for each child at the beginning of the year, with several copies. Design some lessons each week to make sure that all children participate; using the checklist assists in meeting this goal. Be sure that lesson objectives include at least one activity in which all children can achieve an established degree of success. Plan cooperative learning activities so that children with different learning styles can participate comfortably and actively. Multicultural teachers want to avoid consistent interaction with some children throughout the day and inconsistent or nonexistent interaction with others. Thought and planning help them avoid this.

Verbal Discipline

Children attend school to learn, to solve problems, to make mistakes, and to learn from them in a positive environ-ment. Some children exhibit consistent cooperative behaviors, while others are a daily challenge to the patience of teachers. The multicultural classroom transmits the message each day to each child that the opportunity exists to change and to improve under the direction of an understanding teacher. No matter how difficult a child may have been yesterday, an observer the next morning should not detect a tone of annoyance in the teacher's voice when speaking to that student. All children should receive the same warnings, the same clearly expressed expectations, the same encouragement to meet expectations, and the same opportunity to save face and improve behavior after a reprimand or punishment.

The teacher in the multicultural classroom can have an established manner of verbal discipline—one that assumes that the child has the right to change and to exhibit appropriate behavior again as soon as possible. When a child is misbehaving, the following pattern can be effective and equitable:

1. Tell the child exactly what he or she is doing wrong. ("You are speaking while I am speaking.")

2. Tell the child exactly what you expect. ("I want you to listen to my directions so you can work effectively with your group.")

3. Tell the child you believe he or she is capable of successful cooperation. ("I know you can do this!")

If teachers make a decision to remove a child from the group ("You must now sit in the time-out chair."), they should establish an opportunity for the child to return to the group with full privileges restored.

CONCLUSION

This chapter has discussed many ways beyond the established curriculum in which classrooms can successfully demonstrate a multicultural climate. Children must be encouraged, accepted, and valued as individuals before they can extend the same feelings toward others. All schools, within the fullest possible range of racial, cultural, and socioeconomic diversity, can be positive places when they are filled with teachers skilled in building a multicultural climate.

REFERENCES

Bordieu, P., and Passeron, J. C. *Reproduction in Education, Society and Culture,* translated by Richard Nice. Beverly Hills, Calif.: Sage, 1977.

Boyer, J. B. *Multicultural Education: Product or Process?* Kansas City: Kansas Urban Education Center, 1985.

Cuban, L. *To Make a Difference: Teaching in the Inner City.* New York: Free Press, 1970.

Dewey, J. *How We Think.* Lexington, Mass.: D. C. Heath, 1933. P. 59.

Edelman, M. W. "Children At Risk." In *Caring for America's Children,* edited by F. J. Macchiarola and A. Gartner, 20–30. New York: Academy of Political Science, 1989.

Fennimore, B. S. *Child Advocacy for Early Childhood Educators.* New York: Teachers College Press, 1989.

————."Urban Education: An Intervention Strategy." Unpublished manuscript, 1991.

Natriello, G.; McDill, E. L.; and Pallas, A. M. *Schooling Disadvantaged Children: Racing Against Catastrophe.* New York: Teachers College Press, 1989.

Oakes, J. *Keeping Track: How Schools Structure Inequality.* New Haven: Yale University Press, 1985.

Ramsey, P. G. *Teaching and Learning in a Diverse World: Multicultural Education for Young Children.* New York: Teachers College Press, 1987.

Smith, M. M. "Excellence and Equity for America's Children." In *Early Childhood Education 90/91,* edited by J. S. McGee and K. M. Paciorek, 12–17. Guilford, Conn.: Dushkin, 1989.

TEACHER RESOURCES FOR MULTICULTURAL EARLY CHILDHOOD EDUCATION

Many curriculum resources with a multicultural perspective are available for teachers. Some of the resources provide only a philosophical understanding of multicultural education and its development over a 40-year period; others are activity-oriented with learning activities that can be used in early childhood and elementary classroom education environments. The resources in this monograph vary in that some have focused on particular bodies of knowledge or sets of skills, while others have a combined focus on bodies of knowledge interacting with the socio/cultural/developmental context of the learner.

The process of locating multicultural resources for the early childhood classroom can be an exciting adventure. It can also be quite frustrating when there are few indices of where to begin. These teacher resources contain bibliographies of nonstereotypic, antibias materials and instructional programs/activities with a multicultural perspective appropriate for children in early childhood settings. Teachers beginning a multicultural program or attempting to maintain a multicultural perspective in their classrooms will find these sources invaluable.

RESOURCE BOOKS

†* Baker, Gwendolyn C. *Planning and Organizing for Multicultural Instruction.* Reading, Mass.: Addison-Wesley, 1983.

†* Banks, James A. *Teaching Strategies for Ethnic Studies.* Boston: Allyn and Bacon, 1987.

* Banks, James A., and Banks, Cherry A. McGee. *Multicultural Education: Issues and Perspectives.* Boston: Allyn and Bacon, 1989.

* Boyer, James B. *Multicultural Education: Product or Process?* Kansas City: Kansas Urban Education Center, 1985.

Key: * = Multicultural Philosophy; † = Multicultural Activities; ‡ = Resource

†* Chu-Chang, M., ed. *Asian and Pacific American Perspectives in Bilingual Education*. New York: Teachers College Press, 1983.

‡ Dames, Suzanne. "Massasoit, Moccasins, and Massacres: Teaching Anti-Biased Native American Curriculum." Unpublished document, 1988.

‡ Derman-Sparks, Louise, and ABC Task Force. *Anti-Bias Curriculum: Tools for Empowering Young Children*. Washington, D.C.: National Association for the Education of Young Children, 1989.

†* Kendall, Frances E. *Diversity in the Classroom: A Multicultural Approach to the Education of Young Children*. New York: Teachers College Press, 1983.

† Ramsey, P. G.; Vold, E. B.; and Williams, L. R. *Multicultural Education: A Source Book*. New York: Garland, 1989.

‡†* Ramsey, Patricia G. *Teaching and Learning in a Diverse World: Multicultural Education for Young Children*. New York: Teachers College Press, 1987.

‡ Schmidt, Velma E., and McNeil, Earldene. *Cultural Awareness: A Resource Bibliography*. Washington, D.C.: National Association for the Education of Young Children, 1978.

† Tiedt, Pamela, and Tiedt, Iris. *Multicultural Teaching: A Handbook of Activities, Information, and Resources*. Boston: Allyn and Bacon, 1986.

†* Williams, Leslie R.; De Gaetano, Yvonne; Harrington, C. C.; and Sutherland, I. R. *ALERTA*. Menlo Park, Calif.: Addison-Wesley, 1985.

ADDITIONAL RESOURCES

Books for Children Bulletin
Council on Interracial Books for Children, Inc.
1841 Broadway
New York, NY 10023

Multiethnic Books for Young Children
National Association for the Education of Young Children
1834 Connecticut Avenue, NW
Washington, DC 20009

Third World Press
7524 South Cottage Grove
Chicago, IL 60619